The Irish Kitchen

First published in 2008 by

The Appletree Press Ltd
The Old Potato Station
14 Howard Street South
Belfast BT7 1AP

Tel: +44 (028) 90 24 30 74
Fax: +44 (028) 90 24 67 56
Email: reception@appletree.ie
Web: www.appletree.ie

Copyright © Appletree Press, 2008
Text by John Murphy and Marion Maxwell
Photographs as acknowledged on page 93

A catalogue record for this book is available from the British Library.

The Irish Kitchen

ISBN: 978-1-84758-062-7

Desk and Marketing Editor: Jean Brown
Designer: Stuart Wilkinson
Production Manager: Paul McAvoy

9 8 7 6 5 4 3 2 1

AP3467

The Irish Kitchen

John Murphy and
Marion Maxwell

Contents

Introduction

I make no claims that this small book will give the reader anything more than a taste of Ireland. I do not, and indeed cannot, pretend that it is a comprehensive collection of traditional Irish recipes nor do I attempt to define, if it were even possible, an Irish cuisine. All I say is that if a visitor to Ireland were to encounter only what is in this book during a short stay then he would be satisfied that he had eaten well in the Irish style.

Rather then, it is a collection of some favourite traditional Irish dishes which are typical of the cuisine of Ireland. The variety and richness of Irish baking is also looked at as is the baking of breads and cakes which has always been central to our traditions of home and hearth. Happily, home baking skills are still flourishing, thanks to the pride we take in being known for our ready hospitality. This little book charts our baking repertoire from the oatcakes and soda breads that were for so long an essential part of the staple diet, to richer fare that includes festive specialities, up-to-date favourites and cherished family recipes that have stood the test of time.

BREAKFAST
DISHES

Irish Farmhouse Breakfast

I have fond memories of a particularly sunny summer a year or two ago when I stayed in a farmhouse on the Dingle peninsula. As well as the good weather I remember the breakfasts.

Start off with a freshly-cut half grapefruit with a dusting of superfine sugar, followed by a bowl of smooth oatmeal porridge gently cooked in milk and served with an individual jug of cream. After that comes rashers, sausages and eggs, the lot served with scones and brown bread warm from the oven, honey, home-made preserves, fresh butter and a pot of tea. Quantities given are for one person.

2 sausages
1 slice of black pudding
1 slice of white pudding
2 rashers of bacon
2 eggs
a few mushrooms
half a tomato
1 slice of potato bread
baked beans (optional)

Gently fry two sausages over a low heat until well cooked through and golden brown on the outside. Also fry a couple of slices each of black and white pudding. Remove from the pan and keep hot.

Drain off the fat, as it is somewhat indigestible, and fry two rashers of bacon, having first cut off the rind. Now fry a couple of eggs in the bacon fat, spooning the hot fat over the yolks to set them. Heat beans gently if using and keep warm.

Fry a few mushrooms, half a tomato and a slice or two of potato bread each. Add a pat of butter if there is not sufficient bacon fat, but do not cook in butter alone as it burns at too low a temperature. Serve immediately.

A Pot of Tea

It is easy to make a poor cup of tea. Float a tea bag in some milk, pour in some nearly boiling water, mash the tea bag against the side of the cup with a spoon, fish out the tea bag and throw it away. There you are. Awful!

Tea should be made with freshly drawn, freshly boiled water in a warmed pot and allowed to brew. The result will be a pleasant, refreshing drink. To make a good pot of tea, bring freshly drawn water to a brisk boil.

Pour a little into a 1 litre/2 pint earthenware teapot to warm it, then empty the water out. Using good quality loose tea, put 3-5 teaspoons, according to taste, into the warmed pot. Bring the water back to the boil and pour on immediately. Cover the pot with a tea-cosy and allow to brew for 5 minutes – any shorter and the flavour will not have developed, any longer and the tannin will start to come out, making the tea taste stewed. For the same reason, boiling water should be used to make the tea but the brew should not subsequently be boiled.

Potato Bread

Also known as tattie bread, fadge or potato cake, this is delicious hot from the griddle or pan with melted butter and a sprinkling of sugar. It is also a much-loved part of a traditional farmhouse breakfast.

225g/8oz warm cooked potato
½ tsp salt
25g/1oz butter, melted
50g/2oz plain flour

Makes 8

Mash potatoes well. Add salt and butter, then work in enough flour to make a pliable dough. Divide the dough in two and roll out on a floured surface to form two circles 22cm/9inch in diameter and ½cm/¼inch in thickness.

Cut each circle into quarters (called farls) and bake on a hot griddle or pan for about 5 minutes or until browned on both sides. Some people like to grease the baking surface with bacon fat, while others prefer a light dusting of flour for a drier effect.

Pratie Oaten

This is a tasty, textured variation on Potato Bread.

225g/8oz warm cooked potato
½ tsp salt
25g/1oz butter, melted
50g/2oz fine oatmeal

Makes 8

Mash potatoes well. Add salt and butter, then work in enough flour to make a pliable dough. Divide the dough in two and roll out on a floured surface to form two circles 22cm/9inch in diameter and ½cm/¼inch in thickness.

Cut each circle into quarters and bake on a hot griddle or pan for about 5 minutes or until browned on both sides. Some people like to grease the baking surface, while others prefer a light dusting of flour for a drier effect.

Oatcakes

Oats are one of our oldest native crops. These unleavened cakes, also known as strones in Ulster and bannocks in Scotland, were traditionally eaten spread with butter. They were baked on the griddle, then dried out on ornamental "harnen" stands. Delicious with cheese or honey.

25g/1oz plain flour
pinch salt
pinch baking soda
110g/4oz medium oatmeal
25g/1oz butter, margarine or bacon fat
¼ cup boiling water

Makes 4

Sift the flour, salt and baking soda into the oatmeal. Melt the butter, margarine or fat in boiling water and add to the dry ingredients. Mix until the mixture is a spongy mass (a little extra water can be used if necessary). Turn mixture on to a surface covered with plenty of dry oatmeal and scatter more on top. Flatten the dough and roll out until ½cm/¼inch in thickness, then place a dinner plate on top and trim into a neat circle. Scatter on more oatmeal and rub it in all over the surface. Cut into quarters before baking on either a griddle or in the oven.

Griddle method: Place the oatcakes on a heated griddle or heavy pan over medium heat and bake until they dry out and curl. Then place under a grill at medium heat to cook the top of the oatcakes.

Oven method: Bake at gas mark 4, 180°C, 350°F, for 20-30 minutes or until dried out.

Soda Bread

When white flour became widely available, this bread became the mainstay of daily baking in Ireland – and there is still no better way to set off the taste of home-made jam. A friend of mine still makes soda bread in a bastable pot oven inside her gas cooker, but I have found that a heavy cast-iron casserole dish with a lid is equally effective. This bread rises up beautifully and the crust is well-formed but not hard. It is also called oven soda.

450g/1lb plain white flour
1 tsp (heaped) baking soda
1 tsp salt
340-400ml/12-14fl oz buttermilk

Preheat oven to gas mark 6, 200°C, 400°F, and warm an 18cm/7inch cast-iron, lidded casserole dish.

Sift dry ingredients into a large mixing bowl, make a well in the centre and gradually add the buttermilk until all the flour has been incorporated.

Turn the dough out on to a floured surface and knead lightly, then form into a smooth round. Dust the inside of the casserole dish with flour and place the dough inside. Score a deep cross into the top of the dough.

Cover and bake for approximately 50-55 minutes or until the bottom sounds hollow when tapped. Turn out and wrap in a cloth until cold.

Soda Farls

This bread is popular throughout Ireland. Because it is easily and quickly made it is often baked fresh for tea or even breakfast. Before the advent of the bastable oven or the range, most bread was baked on a griddle, swung over the fire or set on a trivet. Rolled thin for ease of baking, griddle bread is traditionally cut in four "farls" or quarters. The soda farl has remained popular, not least as part of an Ulster Fry. If you don't have a griddle, a heavy frying pan or an electric pan will do equally well.

450g/1lb plain white flour
1 tsp (heaped) baking soda
1 tsp salt
340-400ml/12-14fl oz buttermilk

Sift dry ingredients into a large mixing bowl, make a well in the centre and gradually add the buttermilk until all the flour has been incorporated. Turn the dough out on to a floured surface and knead lightly, then form into a smooth round. Cut into quarters.

Place the farls on a moderately hot griddle and cook slowly over a gentle heat until they have risen and a white skin has formed on top, approximately 5-8 minutes. Turn over and cook underside until browned. When cooked the farls will sound hollow if tapped.

Apple Jelly

This well-flavoured jelly is very easy to make and will keep – if given a chance. It is delicious on hot, buttered scones or pancakes. The secret lies in the long, slow cooking which extracts the maximum amount of pectin – the setting agent – from the fruit. To ensure a clear, bright jelly it is vital to resist manfully the temptation to squeeze the pulp when straining the liquid.

2kg/5lb apples
12 whole cloves
2 litres/4 pints water
2kg/4lb sugar

Wash and quarter the apples. There is no need to peel or core them. Place in an ovenproof dish and add water. Cover, with aluminium foil if necessary. Cook overnight at the bottom of the oven, gas mark ½, 225°F, 110°C. Next day strain through a jelly bag or a clean, white pillow case – do not squeeze!

Measure the liquid into a large saucepan and for every cupful add a cupful of sugar. Heat to dissolve the sugar and bring to the boil for about 10 minutes or until a little of the mixture gels on a cold saucer. Be careful here, as over-boiling will produce a syrup which will just get thicker without setting.

Pour into jars which have been warmed in the oven and cover with waxed discs and lids.

SOUPS AND STARTERS

Potato Soup

The basis of a good soup – especially a simple soup such as this – is a good stock. The soup should be made with a white stock, that is, water in which a chicken, ham or bacon has been boiled. Alternatively, stock can be made from a ham bone or chicken carcass boiled with a few root vegetables and herbs as available, and an onion. The stock should be drained, allowed to cool and the fat removed from the surface.

6 medium potatoes
2 medium onions
3 pints/1½ litres stock or milk and water mixed
1 tbsp butter
parsley
salt and pepper

Peel and dice the potatoes and chop the onions. Melt the butter and gently cook the onions and potatoes in a covered saucepan until soft but not coloured.

Add the liquid, adjust the seasoning to taste, sieve if wished and serve in bowls decorated with a little chopped parsley.

Pea and Ham Soup

This soup is made with dried peas; these generally have to be soaked overnight, though it is possible to buy some that need only a few hours' immersion. It is slightly less trouble to make the soup with split peas – which have no skins – and here there is a choice of green or yellow. Although there is no difference in the taste, the latter give the soup a pleasant golden colour.

500g/1lb dried peas or split peas
125g/4oz diced pieces of cooked ham or a ham bone
1 large onion and a little fat (optional)
3 pints/1½ litres ham stock or water
cream (optional)
parsley (optional)
seasoning

Soak the peas as directed on the packet. Chop the onion, if used, and soften in a little fat over a low heat. Add the peas and water or stock and the ham bone if used.

Cook gently until the peas are soft – about an hour. Remove the bone and strip off any meat. This should be cut into small dice and reserved. Purée the peas in a blender or pass through a sieve. Adjust the seasoning. Add the diced ham and serve with a swirl of cream or a sprinkling of chopped parsley on top.

Mutton Broth

It is a good idea to make this broth a day in advance. The fat that rises to the surface will solidify and can easily be removed.

2lb neck of mutton
6 cups water
2 tbsp pearl barley
1 large onion
1 medium turnip
2 large carrots
½ small white cabbage

Put the meat in a large pan and cover with the cold water. Bring to the boil and skim the surface. Rinse the barley and add to the pan.

Cover, but not too tightly, and simmer gently for 90 minutes. Shred the cabbage and dice the other vegetables and add these to the soup. Bring back to the boil and simmer for another hour.

Remove the mutton and separate the meat from any bones, fat or gristle. Chop the meat and return to the soup. Allow to cool and remove fat. Reheat and serve.

Dublin Bay Prawns

The Dublin Bay prawn is otherwise known as the Skye prawn or langoustine. Although the following is not a traditional recipe this delicious sharp-tasting sauce provides the perfect accompaniment for the prawns.

150ml/¼ pint mayonnaise
2 tsp tomato purée
pinch of paprika
dash tabasco
pepper
450g/1lb king prawns
1 tbsp double cream
1 lemon

Mix together mayonnaise, tomato purée, paprika and tabasco. Season to taste. Boil prawns in salted water for 2 minutes only. Remove and shell.

Fold cream into sauce mixture and serve with prawns. Garnish with wedges of lemon and whole (unshelled) prawns.

FISH DISHES

Baked Salmon

There is no doubt that this is an expensive dish, but it will feed eight to ten people and makes a fine party piece.

1 fresh salmon (about 5lb/ 2kg)
parsley
salt and pepper
½ cup butter
½ cup dry cider
250ml/½ pint double cream

Clean and descale the salmon, cut off the head and tail and trim the fins. Stuff the parsley into the gullet. Butter some aluminium foil and form a loose envelope round the fish, sealing both ends but leaving the top open for the moment.

Dot the rest of the butter over the salmon, season and pour over the cider and the cream. Now seal the foil along the top, leaving only a small vent. Bake in the oven for 1¼ hours at gas mark 4, 350°F, 180°C.

When ready, take from the oven, remove the skin and reduce the sauce by boiling, stirring all the time. Serve with boiled new potatoes and fresh garden peas.

Dublin Lawyer

This dish is delicious and traditional – a happy combination – though its expensive ingredients make it a rare treat rather than an everyday affair. For the best flavour the fish has to be freshly killed just before cooking. Plunge a sharp knife into the cross on the back of the head. Slice in half lengthwise and crack open the claws. Remove all the flesh and cut into large chunks. Keep both halves of the shell for serving.

1 live lobster, about 1kg/2lb
125g/4oz butter
150ml/¼ pint Irish whiskey
150ml/¼ pint whipping cream
salt and pepper

Toss the lobster meat in foaming butter over a medium heat for a few minutes until cooked. Take care that the butter does not burn.

Add the whiskey and when it has heated up set light to it. Pour in the cream, heat through and season. Serve in the half shells with plainly boiled fine beans.

Salmon Steaks

The king of fish requires very little in the way of addition or garnishing. Here is a simple recipe.

4 slices salmon (about 2 cm/¾ inch thick)
2 tbsp melted butter
salt and pepper
parsley
lemon, sliced

Wipe the salmon slices with a damp cloth and brush over with melted butter. Season with salt and pepper on both sides.

Place the slices under a hot grill. Grill each side for 5 minutes or so, as necessary. Serve garnished with parsley and sliced lemon.

Parsley Sauce

This simple Parsley Sauce is an ideal accompaniment to fish.

25g/1oz butter
25g/1oz plain flour
575ml/1 pint milk
seasoning
1 tbsp finely chopped parsley

Melt the butter; add the flour and stir with a wooden spoon over a gentle heat for around a minute. Slowly add the milk, then bring to the boil and season to taste, stirring continuously.

Add the finely chopped parsley and simmer gently for 5 minutes. Pour into a sauceboat and serve hot.

MAIN COURSE
DISHES

Champ

Champ is a simple warming dish which is cheap, easy to produce and very filling. When I was a child we used to have it at Hallowe'en for dinner. A silver sixpenny piece wrapped in greaseproof paper would be buried in it. To find it in your portion was to bring good luck for a year – quite apart from the temporary wealth.

8 medium potatoes, peeled
small bunch of scallions (spring onions)
125ml/¼ pint milk
salt and pepper
knob of butter per person

The best way to prepare the potatoes is to cook them in a steamer and then pass them through a food mill. Alternatively, boil until soft but not mushy, drain and return them to the heat to dry somewhat before mashing. In any case keep hot.

Chop the scallions finely, both green and white parts, and cook for 5 minutes in the milk. Beat this mixture into the mashed potatoes until smooth and fluffy, season to taste and serve a large mound on each plate with a good knob of butter melting into the top. Each forkful is dipped into the melted butter as it is eaten. Very good with a glass of cold milk.

Colcannon is made in much the same way as champ, but with the addition of cabbage. In parts of the country white cabbage is always used. In any case, shred and chop a small cabbage (discard the stump) and cook until tender. Beat into the potato mixture and serve as above.

Spiced Beef

Spiced beef is traditionally eaten at Christmas time. It tends to be rather expensive to buy as it is quite labour intensive to make, though it uses a modestly enough priced cut. It can be made at home, but it does take time.

3kg/7lb even-sized piece of topside or silverside
2 tsp each ground cloves, milled black pepper,
    allspice, cinnamon, mace and saltpetre
2 tbsp black treacle
2 tbsp brown sugar
cold water to cover
bottle Guinness
125g/4oz salt

Combine all the ingredients except the beef, water and Guinness. Place the beef in a bowl and cover with the mixture. Rub it in once or twice a day for a week.

Tie up the meat into a good shape and place in a pan. Cover with cold water to which a bottle of Guinness has been added. Simmer gently for 5-6 hours. Remove from liquid. When cool, press lightly between two plates. The beef is usually served cold, thinly sliced.

Corned Beef and Cabbage

Corned beef is brisket, topside or silverside which has been pickled in brine. It is especially popular around Dublin. It is best to soak a joint overnight to remove excess salt.

2kg/5lb joint of corned beef
1 large cabbage
2 large onions
2 large carrots
4 potatoes
cold water to cover
bay leaf
ground black pepper

Quarter the cabbage and put aside. Peel and slice the other vegetables. Cover the meat with the water and bring to the boil. Skim the surface, add the vegetables (except the cabbage), the bay leaf and the pepper and simmer gently for 20 minutes. Add the cabbage and cook for a further 30 minutes.

Serve the meat surrounded by the vegetables with additional mashed potatoes.

Baked Limerick Ham

To the Irish, ham is a cured leg of pork. The preserving process is carried out in a number of different ways: salting, smoking, immersion in brine or even honey. Traditionally, Limerick ham is smoked over juniper branches. Whole hams should be steeped in cold water overnight before cooking but this is not necessary with smaller joints. The ham in this recipe is not really baked but rather finished off in the oven after having been cooked by simmering in cider.

1½-2kg/3-5lb ham
cider to cover
125g/4oz brown sugar
1 tsp mustard
20 whole cloves

Cover the ham with cold water and bring slowly to the boil. Throw out the water and replace with cider. Bring this just to the boil and lower the heat, keeping the liquid barely simmering for 20 minutes to the 1 lb/ ½ kg. Remove from the heat and allow to stand in the liquid for 30 minutes.

Take out the ham, skin it and score the fat with a sharp knife in a diamond pattern. Stud with whole cloves. Mix the sugar and mustard and rub well into the surface of the ham. Bake in a pre-heated oven for a further 10 minutes to the 1lb/ ½ kg at gas mark 6, 400°F, 200°C.

Beef in Guinness

The Guinness in this recipe has the same function as the wine in Coq Au Vin – the acid and moisture combined with the long, slow cooking help tenderise the tough but flavoursome meat.

1kg/2½lb shin of beef
2 large onions
6 medium carrots
2 tbsp seasoned flour
a little fat or beef dripping
250ml/½ pint Guinness and water mixed
sprig of parsley

Cut the beef into chunks and peel and slice the onions and carrots. Toss the beef in the flour and brown quickly in hot fat. Remove the beef and fry the onions gently until transparent. Return the beef and add the carrots and the liquid.

Bring just to the boil, reduce the heat to a very gentle simmer, cover closely and cook for 1½-2 hours. Check that the dish does not dry out, adding more liquid if necessary. Sprinkle with chopped parsley and serve with plainly boiled potatoes.

Irish Stew

Irish stew is easy to make and if made with mutton and cooked slowly will be both flavoursome and tender. Mutton, being an older meat, has more flavour than lamb but does need to be cooked for a couple of hours over a low heat with liquid. It should not be allowed to boil or the flavour will be spoiled. There is little agreement as to the classic recipe – should there be carrots? Should the meat be browned? Should mutton, lamb, beef, bacon or even kid be used? The following dish will be found to be hearty and nourishing and traditional enough.

1kg/2½lb boned mutton
4 large potatoes
2 large onions
3 or 4 medium carrots
sprig of parsley
500ml/1 pint water
salt and pepper

Cut the meat into good size chunks. Peel the vegetables and slice thickly. Chop the parsley. Choose a pot with a well-fitting lid and put in the ingredients in layers, starting and finishing with potatoes. Pour in the water and season to taste.

Cover and put on a very low heat for about 2½ hours until the meat is tender and the potatoes have thickened the liquid. The dish may also be made with lamb, in which case it requires only 1½ hours cooking time.

Dublin Coddle

This is a very popular dish, especially in Dublin, and has been so for many years. It is nourishing, tasty, economical and warming – what more could you ask? Although it is best made with a good stock – water in which a ham has been boiled, or even a ham bone – a light stock cube will substitute.

500g/1lb best sausages
250g/8oz streaky bacon
300ml/½ pint stock or water
6 medium potatoes
2 medium onions
salt and pepper

Cut the bacon into 1 inch/ 3 cm squares. Bring the stock to the boil in a medium saucepan which has a well-fitting lid, add the sausages and the bacon and simmer for about 5 minutes. Remove the sausages and bacon and save the liquid.

Cut each sausage into four or five pieces. Peel the potatoes and cut into thick slices. Skin the onions and slice them. Assemble a layer of potatoes in the saucepan, followed by a layer of onions and then half the sausages and bacon.

Repeat the process once more and then finish off with a layer of potatoes. Pour the reserved stock over and season lightly to taste.

Cover and simmer gently for about an hour. Adjust the seasoning and serve piping hot.

Boxty

Boxty is a traditional potato dish, celebrated in the rhyme:

Boxty on the griddle,
Boxty in the pan,
If you can't make boxty,
You'll never get your man

250g/8oz raw potato
250g/8oz mashed potato
250g/8oz plain flour
1 tsp baking powder
1 tsp salt
large knob of butter, melted
about 125ml/¼ pint milk

Grate the raw potatoes into a bowl. Turn out onto a cloth and wring, catching the liquid. This will separate into a clear fluid with starch at the bottom. Pour off the fluid and scrape out the starch and mix with the grated and mashed potatoes.

Sieve the dry ingredients and mix in along with the melted butter. Add a little milk if necessary to make a pliable dough. Knead lightly on a floured surface. Divide into four and form large, flat cakes.

Mark each into quarters but do not cut right through, and bake on a griddle or in a heavy pan. Serve immediately spread with butter or reheat later by frying the farls with bacon.

If liked, more milk and an egg can be added to make a batter which can be fried in bacon fat like drop scones.

BREADS, SCONES AND PANCAKES

Wheaten Bread

Ask Irish emigrés what they miss about home and it's likely they will name wheaten bread as one of the things they hanker for. Conventionally, it is a variant on white soda bread made with half wholemeal flour, but this version uses all wholemeal enriched with wheatgerm, bran and oats. It needs no kneading, slices well and is delicious with smoked salmon, cheese or honey.

110g/4oz plain white flour
3 tsp (level) baking soda
½ to ¾ tsp salt
275g/10oz coarse wholemeal flour
275g/10oz fine wholemeal flour
2 tbsp wheatgerm
80g/3oz pinhead or rolled oats
2 tbsp bran
1 tbsp (scant) brown sugar
50g/2oz butter, margarine (or 2-2½ tbsp olive oil)
825ml/1½ pint buttermilk

Preheat oven to gas mark 6, 200°C, 400°F, and grease and flour two 900g/2lb loaf tins.

Sieve plain flour with baking soda and salt. Stir in other dry ingredients and rub in butter or margarine (or stir in the olive oil.) Gradually add the buttermilk until the mixture is slack enough to spoon into the tins.

Place in the oven and bake for 50-60 minutes. To test if the wheaten is cooked through, tap on the bottom, if it sounds hollow it is ready. Cover with a cloth until cold. This bread freezes well.

Potato Apple Cake

If you are trying this for the first time, you will soon realise why it has long been considered the highlight of a farmhouse tea. Be sure to cook it until the apples are soft and don't stint on the sugar and butter which melt into a delicious sauce at the end. Traditionally, at Hallowe'en, a ring would be hidden in the filling for luck.

225g/8oz warm cooked potato
½ tsp salt
25g/1oz butter, melted
50g/2oz plain flour
275g/10oz Bramley apples, peeled and thinly sliced
butter and sugar to taste

Makes 2

Mash potatoes well. Add salt and butter, then work in enough flour to make a pliable dough. Divide the potato dough in two and roll each half into a circle about 20cm/8inch in diameter.

Arrange the apples on half of each circle, then fold over to form pastie shapes and crimp around the edges to give a good seal. Cook as for potato bread in a heavy pan or on the griddle, turning half-way through. Brown slowly to ensure that the apples have time to soften, approximately 20 minutes.

Gently slit open the cakes and insert slivers of butter and plenty of sugar. Reseal and return to heat for 5 minutes, to allow the sauce to form.

Yeast Bread With Stout

This is my version of the time-honoured beer bread, made in celebration of stout – the dark brew that has become associated the world over with Ireland. The recipe is fail-safe, ideal for those not too familiar with yeast cookery.

1 tbsp (heaped) soft brown sugar
275ml/10fl oz stout
50g/2oz butter
25g/1oz fresh yeast
1 tsp (level) salt
1 egg, beaten
225g/8oz wholemeal flour
225g/8oz strong white flour
1 tsp ground ginger (optional)
1 tsp caraway seeds (optional)

Preheat oven to gas mark 5, 190°C, 375°F, and grease a 900g/2lb loaf tin.

Place sugar, stout and butter in a large saucepan and bring to boil, then cool until lukewarm. Add a spoonful of this liquid to the yeast and mix until creamy. Add yeast, salt and egg to the stout mixture.

Sift flour into a large, warmed, mixing bowl, with ginger and caraway seeds. Make a well in the centre of the dry ingredients and add liquid. Mix with a knife, then your fingers until it forms a soft dough. Knead for 10 minutes until smooth, elastic, and a little shiny.

Return dough to bowl and cover with oiled clingfilm. Leave in a warm place until the dough has doubled in size. Then knead again until smooth, put in loaf tin, cover and set aside to prove a second time.

When dough has doubled in bulk again, put in oven and bake for about 35 minutes. Bread is ready if it sounds hollow when tapped.

Buttermilk Scones

Morning coffee and afternoon tea would not be complete without fresh scones and there are so many delicious varieties. The secret of making good scones is a quick, light hand when mixing and a hot oven. Scones are best baked fresh as they go stale very quickly.

225g/8oz self-raising soda bread flour
pinch salt
25g/1oz butter or hard margarine
1 egg, beaten
140ml/5fl oz buttermilk
egg or milk to glaze (optional)

Makes 8

Preheat oven to gas mark 8, 230°C, 450°F.
    Sift flour with salt and rub in butter or margarine. Make a well in the centre and pour in the egg and most of the buttermilk. Mix quickly to form a soft dough, adding a little extra buttermilk if necessary.
    Turn out on to a floured surface and roll out lightly until 2.5cm/1inch in thickness. Working quickly, cut into 5cm/2inch rounds. Glaze with egg or milk and set on a floured baking sheet.
    Bake for 15-20 minutes until light brown.

For **Fruit Scones** add a tablespoonful of superfine sugar and two tablespoonfuls of dried fruit before adding the milk.

Savoury Cheese and Herb Scones

These tasty scones are an ideal accompaniment to soup or a summer salad.

225g/8oz self-raising soda bread flour
1 tsp dry mustard
pinch salt
25g/1oz butter or hard margarine
1 egg, beaten
140ml/5fl oz buttermilk
egg or milk to glaze (optional)
extra grated cheese (optional)

Makes 8

Preheat oven to gas mark 8, 230°C, 450°F.

Sift flour with the mustard and salt then rub in butter or margarine. Stir in the chopped herbs and grated cheese (retaining a tablespoon of cheese). Make a well in the centre and pour in the egg and most of the buttermilk. Mix quickly to form a soft dough, adding a little extra buttermilk if necessary.

Turn out on to a floured surface and roll out lightly until 2.5cm/1inch in thickness. Working quickly, cut into 5cm/2inch rounds. Glaze with egg or milk and if wished scatter a little grated cheese on the top of each scone.

Set on a floured baking sheet and bake for 15-20 minutes until light brown.

Wheaten Scones

These are staple fare in my home, eaten with butter and honey.
Many versions use half white flour but all wholemeal makes for
a nuttier scone, further enhanced by the use of molasses-rich
sugar.

450g/1lb coarse wholemeal flour
pinch salt
1 tsp (heaped) baking soda
1 tsp (heaped) cream of tartar
80g/3oz dark muscovado sugar
50g/2oz butter or margarine
2 eggs, beaten
175ml/6fl oz buttermilk

Makes 8

Preheat oven to gas mark 8, 220°C, 450°F, and grease a
baking sheet.
　　Sieve flour with salt, baking soda and cream of tartar,
returning the bran left in the sieve to the flour. Rub in sugar and
fat and make a well in the middle of the dry mixture. Add the
eggs and most of the buttermilk, incorporating it quickly and
lightly and adding extra, if necessary, to form a soft dough.
　　Roll out on a floured surface until 2.5cm/1inch in thickness,
cut into rounds about 5cm/2inch in diameter. Place on a
greased baking sheet and bake for 15-20 minutes.

Date Scones

This is a delicious variation on the basic wheaten scone recipe.

340g/12oz wholemeal flour
175g/6oz white flour
pinch salt
1 tsp (heaped) baking soda
1 tsp (heaped) cream of tartar
80g/3oz dark muscovado sugar
50g/2oz butter or margarine
110g/4oz chopped dates
2 eggs, beaten
175ml/6fl oz buttermilk

Makes 8

Preheat oven to gas mark 8, 220°C, 450°F, and grease a baking sheet.

Sieve flours together with salt, baking soda and cream of tartar, returning the bran left in the sieve to the flour. Rub in sugar and fat. Stir in the chopped dates then make a well in the middle of the dry mixture. Add the eggs and most of the buttermilk, incorporating it quickly and lightly and adding extra, if necessary, to form a soft dough.

Roll out on a floured surface until 2.5cm/1inch in thickness, cut into rounds about 5cm/2inch in diameter. Place on a greased baking sheet and bake for 15-20 minutes.

Barm Brack

"Barm" derives either from *bairm* – an early form of ale yeast – or *bairin* meaning cake, while "brack" comes from the Irish *breac* meaning spotted.

25g/1oz fresh yeast
80g/3oz caster sugar
275ml/10fl oz tepid milk
1 egg, beaten
450g/1lb strong white flour
½ tsp cinnamon
¼ tsp grated nutmeg
½ tsp salt
50g/2oz butter
225g/8oz sultanas
110g/4oz currants
50g/2oz mixed peel
2 tbsp sugar dissolved in 2 tbsp hot water to glaze

Cream together the yeast and 1 teaspoon each of the sugar and milk. Mix well then add the remaining milk and the egg. Sieve flour, spices and salt into a mixing bowl, rub in the butter and add the fruit and peel.

Stir in the yeast mixture and beat well with a wooden spoon then, using your hands, form a dough and knead on a floured surface for 10 minutes until the dough becomes elastic. Place in a greased bowl, cover with oiled polythene and leave in a warm place for about an hour.

Divide dough in half and knead each for a few minutes, then place each in a cake tin and return to a warm place for another hour until well risen. Preheat oven to gas mark 6, 200°C, 400°F.

Bake for 30-35 minutes then remove from heat. Dissolve sugar in hot water and glaze while hot.

Whiskey Tea Brack

Tea brack derives its moisture and flavour from the strong, sweet tea in which the fruit is soaked overnight. This is my version of a recipe given to the late Theodora Fitzgibbon by her grandmother who soaked the fruit in a mixture of half tea and half whiskey!

225g/8oz sultanas
225g/8oz raisins
225g/8oz soft brown sugar
½ tsp cinnamon
¼ tsp grated nutmeg
2 tbsp whiskey
275ml/10fl oz strong tea
450g/1lb self-raising flour
2 eggs, beaten
marmalade or honey to glaze
demerara sugar to dust

Place the sultanas, raisins, sugar, cinnamon, nutmeg, whiskey and tea in a large bowl and soak overnight.

Preheat oven to gas mark 3, 160°C, 325°F, and grease and line a 20cm/8inch round cake tin.

Stir in the sieved flour and eggs and mix well. Bake for approximately 1½ hours.

Towards the end of baking time, brush with marmalade or honey and sprinkle with demerara sugar. To test if the brack is cooked insert a skewer into the centre, if it comes out clean then the brack is ready. When cold, slice and butter generously.

Currant Soda

The following three recipes, all enriched forms of basic soda bread, often appear together on the tea table.

450g/1lb plain white flour
1 tsp (heaped) baking soda
1 tsp salt
340-400ml/12-14fl oz buttermilk
50g/2oz caster sugar
25g/1oz butter or margarine
175g/6oz dried fruit
1 egg, beaten (optional)

Preheat oven to gas mark 6, 200°C, 400°F, and warm an 18cm/7inch cast-iron, lidded casserole dish.

Sift dry ingredients into a large mixing bowl. Rub in butter or margarine. Stir in fruit. Make a well in the centre. Add beaten egg, if using, to the buttermilk, and gradually add the buttermilk until all the flour has been incorporated.

Turn the dough out on to a floured surface and knead lightly, then form into a smooth round. Dust the inside of the casserole dish with flour and place the dough inside. Score a deep cross into the top of the dough.

Cover and bake for approximately 50-55 minutes or until the bottom sounds hollow when tapped. Turn out and wrap in a cloth until cold.

Treacle Bread

Treacle is one of those things you either love or hate. If you are one of those people who love it, this recipe is for you.

450g/1lb plain white flour
1 tsp (heaped) baking soda
1 tsp salt
340-400ml/12-14fl oz buttermilk
50g/2oz caster sugar
50g/2oz butter or margarine
50g/2oz sultanas (optional)
2 tbsp treacle
1 egg, beaten
pinch ginger (optional)

Preheat oven to gas mark 6, 200°C, 400°F, and warm an 18cm/7inch cast-iron, lidded casserole dish.

Sift dry ingredients into a large mixing bowl. Add sugar to dry ingredients and rub in butter or margarine. Stir in fruit if using. Add treacle, egg and ginger to buttermilk and gradually add to dry ingredients until all the flour has been incorporated.

Turn the dough out on to a floured surface and knead lightly, then form into a smooth round. Dust the inside of the casserole dish with flour and place the dough inside. Score a deep cross into the top of the dough.

Cover and bake for approximately 50-55 minutes or until the bottom sounds hollow when tapped. Turn out and wrap in a cloth until cold.

Cornmeal Bread

Cornmeal, known as "yalla male" or "india buck", was first imported into Ireland during the Great Famine.

250g/8oz plain white flour
250g/8oz coarse cornmeal
1 tsp (heaped) baking soda
1 tsp salt
340-400ml/12-14fl oz buttermilk

Preheat oven to gas mark 6, 200°C, 400°F, and warm an 18cm/7inch cast-iron, lidded casserole dish.

Sift dry ingredients into a large mixing bowl, make a well in the centre and gradually add the buttermilk until all the flour has been incorporated.

Turn the dough out on to a floured surface and knead lightly, then form into a smooth round. Dust the inside of the casserole dish with flour and place the dough inside. Score a deep cross into the top of the dough.

Cover and bake for approximately 50-55 minutes or until the bottom sounds hollow when tapped. Turn out and wrap in a cloth until cold.

Drop Scones

These are also known as Scotch Pancakes, especially in the north. They must be cooked as soon as possible after mixing, as the acid in the buttermilk starts to react with the baking soda at once. For that reason the griddle or pan should be heated before combining the ingredients.

250g/8oz plain flour
½ tsp baking soda
½ tsp salt
1 tsp sugar
1 large egg
250ml/½ pint buttermilk

Sift the dry ingredients into a bowl. Make a well in the middle with a wooden spoon and add the egg. Break the yolk and pour in the buttermilk, mixing quickly to a thick batter. Do not beat, as this would develop the gluten in the flour and prevent the pancakes from rising.

Fry in large dollops on a lightly-greased, hot griddle or heavy frying pan, turning over when set.

Drop scones are best served hot for tea, thickly spread with melting butter and syrup or jam.

Pancakes

Cooked on the griddle or the pan, these are traditional fare for Shrove Tuesday as they use eggs, milk and butter, all of which were forbidden during a strict Lenten fast. Here is an easy way to make them.

125g/4oz plain flour
pinch of salt
2 eggs
250ml/½ pint milk
1 tbsp melted butter

Put all the ingredients in a blender and blend for about 30 seconds. The batter should then be allowed to stand for 30 minutes in a cool place.

Heat a small frying pan over a medium heat. Grease with a little butter and wipe out with kitchen paper. Fry about 2 tbsp of batter at a time, swirling to cover the base of the pan. Keep them thin and there will be no need to turn.

Serve rolled up with sugar and a squeeze of lemon juice.

CAKES

Boiled Fruit Cake

With the main ingredients quickly measured out in cupfuls (a standard breakfast cup will do) and no creaming or rubbing-in to be done, this cut-and-come-again cake is an established favourite. Delicious sliced and buttered for tea.

1 cup water
225g/8oz butter
1 cup soft brown sugar
½ cup peel
1½ cups raisins
1¼ cups sultanas
¼ cup cherries
1 tsp mixed spice
2 cups flour
1 tsp baking soda
2 eggs, beaten

Put first eight ingredients into a large saucepan and bring to a boil. Simmer gently for 20 minutes, then set aside to cool.

Preheat oven to gas mark 4, 180°C, 350°F, and grease and line a 20cm/8inch cake tin.

Sieve the flour and baking soda into the fruit mixture and add the beaten eggs. Mix well, then turn into a cake tin and bake for 1-1½ hours or until cooked through. (Reduce the temperature towards the end of the cooking time if necessary.)

Cool in the tin for 15 minutes, then turn out on to a rack. This cake will keep well if stored in an airtight tin.

Porter Cake

Porter is a type of dark Irish beer, not now as widely available as it once was. It is not as strong as stout but Guinness, Murphy's or other Irish stout can be substituted in this recipe if mixed fifty-fifty with water. This cake is quickly and easily made and, though it tastes good fresh from the oven, it is best kept for about a week in an airtight tin.

250ml/½ pint porter
250g/8oz butter
250g/8oz brown sugar
1kg /2lb mixed dried fruit
    (equal quantities currants, raisins, sultanas
    with about half as much mixed peel)
500g/1¼lb plain flour
½ tsp baking soda
1 tsp mixed spice
grated rind from one small lemon (optional)
3 medium eggs

Melt the butter and sugar in the porter in a saucepan. Add the fruit and simmer for 10 minutes.

Allow to go cold and add the sieved flour, baking soda, spices and lemon rind. Beat the eggs and mix in with a wooden spoon.

Pour into a greased and lined 9 inch/ 25 cm cake tin and bake on the middle shelf of a pre-heated oven at gas mark 3, 325°F, 160°C for about 1¾ hours. To test the cake, push a skewer into the centre; if ready, the skewer will come out clean.

Allow the cake to cool in the tin.

Guinness Cake

When Arthur Guinness began brewing porter at St James's Gate, Dublin in 1759, he could hardly have envisaged that his distinctive stout would become a household name. This recipe is similar to Porter Cake but features the addition of walnuts to add an extra nuttiness to the flavour.

275g/10oz plain flour
generous ½ tsp baking soda
2 tsp mixed spice
225g/8oz butter or margarine
225g/8oz soft brown sugar
4 eggs, beaten
225g/8oz raisins
225g/8oz sultanas
110g/4oz peel
110g/4oz walnuts, chopped
rind of 1 lemon, grated
5-6fl oz Guinness

Preheat oven to gas mark 3, 170°C, 325°F, and grease and line an 18cm/7inch cake tin.

Sift flour, baking soda and spice into a mixing bowl. In a separate bowl, cream the butter and sugar together until fluffy. Gradually beat in eggs, adding a little flour with each addition.

Fold in the rest of the flour and stir in the fruit, peel, nuts and rind. Pour in half of the Guinness, mix well and pour into the cake tin.

Bake for 1 hour then reduce the temperature to gas mark 2, 150°C, 300°F; cover cake lightly with greaseproof paper and bake for a further 1½ hours. To test if the cake is done insert a skewer; if it comes out clean the cake is ready. Remove from the oven and allow to cool before turning out of the tin.

Prick the cake all over with a skewer or fork and drizzle the remaining Guinness over. Wrap in foil and store for a week before cutting.

Seed Cake

For centuries, caraway seeds have been used to lend a distinctive flavour to puddings, biscuits and cakes. A handful would often be thrown in to speckle a sweetened soda bread. This rich cake, known also as "carvie", recalls days of gracious living in substantial country houses, when visiting ladies would be offered a slice with a glass of port.

275g/10oz flour
½ tsp baking powder
¼ tsp cinnamon
¼ tsp nutmeg
225g/8oz butter
225g/8oz caster sugar
4 eggs, beaten
3 tbsp caraway seeds

Preheat oven to gas mark 3, 160°C, 325°F, and grease and line a 20cm/8inch cake tin.

Sift flour with baking powder, cinnamon and nutmeg. In a separate bowl, cream the butter and sugar together until pale and fluffy, then gradually mix in the eggs, adding a little flour with each addition. Fold in the rest of the flour and mix well.

Reserve a teaspoon of the caraway seeds to decorate the top of the cake and stir the rest into the mixture.

Bake for approximately 1½ hours, until pale gold in colour and firm to the touch.

Featherlight Sponge Cake

This light-as-air cake is often used as a yardstick for judging the best baker in the parish, some of whom will swear by using duck eggs for extra volume. Perfect simply sandwiched with jam and cream, this basic mixture can also be transformed into a swiss roll, a layered gateau or a trifle base.

4 large eggs, separated
110g/4oz caster sugar
110g/4oz self-raising flour, sieved

Preheat oven to gas mark 4, 180°C, 350°F, and grease and line two 18cm/7inch cake tins.

Beat egg yolks and sugar together until very pale and thick, then set aside. In a separate bowl, beat the egg whites until they stand in stiff peaks. Fold the egg whites into the egg and sugar mixture, then gently fold in the flour.

Divide the mixture between the cake tins and bake in the middle of the oven for about 25-30 minutes, until the sponge has shrunk slightly from the sides of the tins and is firm and springy to the touch.

When cold, sandwich together with jam, cream, fresh fruit, lemon curd or a combination of these. Finish with a dusting of caster sugar, or make a pretty pattern by sprinkling icing sugar over a doily set on the cake.

Scripture Cake

This delicious fruit cake is perfect for Sunday tea and for entertaining visitors. The recipe is cleverly devised to send you thumbing through your bible to decipher the ingredients. The results, of course, are divine!

110g/4oz Jeremiah Ch. I v. 11
340g/12oz Jeremiah Ch. XXIV v. 2
340g/12oz I Chronicles Ch. XII v. 40
500g/1lb 2oz Leviticus Ch. II v. 2
2 tsp (level) Galacians Ch. V v. 9
1 tsp (level) Solomon Ch. IV v. 14
pinch St Matthew Ch.V v. 13
6 Job Ch. XXXIX v. 14
340g/12oz Isaiah Ch. VII v. 15
450g/1lb Jeremiah Ch. VI v. 20
½ breakfast cup Solomon Ch. IV v. 11
2 tbsp I Samuel Ch. XIV v. 29

Preheat oven to gas mark 3, 180°C, 350°F, and grease and line a 22cm/9inch cake tin.

Blanch, peel and chop the almonds. Chop the figs. Sift flour with baking powder, cinnamon and salt.

Cream butter and caster sugar until fluffy. Gradually mix in beaten eggs, adding a little flour with each addition. Fold in the rest of the flour along with the honey, milk and fruit.

Turn into tin and bake for approximately 2¼ hours. The cake is ready when a skewer is inserted and comes out clean.

Lemon and Vanilla Curd Cake

Curds were once an important part of the Irish diet, and were also useful for paying the rent. Recipes for this delicately flavoured cheesecake are found in several eighteenth-century "receipt" books.

Pastry:
175g/6oz plain flour
pinch of salt
75g/3oz margarine or butter
25g/1oz caster sugar
1 egg yolk cold water

Filling:
40g/1½oz butter
50g/2oz vanilla flavoured sugar
     (or caster sugar plus essence)
2 egg yolks
1 tbsp (heaped) plain flour
rind and juice of ½ lemon
225g/8oz cottage cheese

Topping:
1 tbsp flour
1 tbsp sugar
1 tbsp butter, melted
1 egg, beaten
caster sugar to dust

Preheat oven to gas mark 4, 180°C, 350°F, warm a baking sheet and grease a loose-bottomed flan tin.

To prepare the pastry sieve flour, salt and sugar into a bowl. Cut up margarine and rub into the flour with tips of fingers until the mixture resembles fine breadcrumbs. Add the yolk, stirring through, then slowly add enough cold water to make a firm dough, mixing with a knife. Turn onto a floured board and knead lightly with finger tips. Roll out the shortcrust pastry until thin, then line the flan tin with the dough, trimming off any excess. Chill pastry case in the fridge.

Cream the butter and sugar together until fluffy, then beat in the egg yolks, flour, lemon rind, lemon juice and sieved cottage cheese. Mix well, then spoon into the pastry case. Mix topping ingredients together and spread on top of the curd filling.

Place the flan tin on the warmed baking sheet and bake for approximately 1 hour or until the top is lightly browned and slightly firm. Dust with caster sugar and serve cool but not chilled.

Irish Chocolate Cake

The "Irishness" of this lovely chocolate cake is thanks not only to the wonderful liqueur used in the filling, but also to a certain, very Irish, ingredient in the cake mixture itself which contributes to its moistness.

Sponge:
175g/6oz self-raising flour
½ tsp salt
50g/2oz dark chocolate
110g/4oz butter
175g/6oz caster sugar
80g/3oz cooked mashed potato
2 eggs, beaten
4 tbsp milk

Filling:
110g/4oz dark chocolate
125ml/4fl oz double cream
50g/2oz icing sugar
3 tbsp Irish cream liqueur

Preheat oven to gas mark 5, 190°C, 375°F, and grease and line two 20cm/8inch cake tins.

Sift flour and salt into a mixing bowl. Melt chocolate in a bowl placed over a saucepan of hot water. In a separate bowl, cream butter and sugar together until fluffy, then beat in the chocolate and mashed potato. Gradually beat in the eggs, adding a little flour with each addition. Fold in the rest of the flour and stir in the milk.

Divide mixture between cake tins and bake for 25-30 minutes or until top is firm but springy to the touch. Remove from oven and after a few minutes, turn out on to a cooling rack. While the cake is cooling make the filling.

To Prepare the Filling:
Melt the chocolate as before, stir in the other ingredients and mix well. Use the filling to sandwich the sponge layers together and coat the top and sides of the cake.

Old-Fashioned Ginger Cake

In ancient times, cakes flavoured with ginger, known as *craebh*, were associated with Midsummer customs: a basket of cakes was placed on a pole and dancers would compete to win them.

110g/4oz butter or margarine
110g/4oz soft brown sugar
3 dsp golden syrup
3 dsp treacle
225g/8oz plain flour
1 tsp baking soda
1 tsp cinnamon
1½ tsp ground ginger
1 egg
3 tbsp buttermilk
50g/2oz crystallised ginger, chopped (optional)

In a saucepan, gently melt the butter, sugar, golden syrup and treacle together, then set aside to cool.

Preheat oven to gas mark 4, 180°C, 350°F, and grease and line a 20cm/8inch cake tin.

Sift flour, soda and spices. Beat egg with buttermilk and mix well into dry ingredients. Reserve a teaspoon of the chopped ginger to decorate, and add the rest to the dry ingredients. Pour into the cake tin and bake for approximately 1 hour.

When the cake is cool decorate with Orange Glacé Icing and the reserved crystallised ginger.

Orange Glacé Icing

This simple water icing is perfect for topping the Old-Fashioned Ginger Cake.

225g/8oz icing sugar
1-2 drops of orange essence
2-3 tbsp boiling water

Sieve the icing sugar into a bowl and add the orange essence. Add the water slowly until you have reached the required consistency.

BISCUITS AND TRAYBAKES

Flakemeal Crunchies

This is an updated version of the ever-popular oat biscuits. The coating of demerara sugar, adds a special crunch and is an inspired touch.

175g/6oz flour
1 tsp baking soda
1 tsp baking powder
175g/6oz caster sugar
110g/4oz butter
110g/4oz white pastry fat
1 egg
110g/4oz rolled oats (flake meal)
50g/2oz Weetabix, crushed
50g/2oz cornflakes, roughly crushed
50g/2oz coconut
80g/3oz demerara sugar

Makes 30

Preheat oven to gas mark 4, 180°C, 350°F, and grease two baking trays. Sift flour, baking soda and baking powder together. Cream together caster sugar, butter and pastry fat. Add egg and mix well, then fold in flour mixture, cereals and coconut.

Shape into balls the size of a large walnut and roll each in demerara sugar. Flatten into rounds, place on baking trays and bake for 20-25 minutes until golden brown.

Currant Squares

Even in the age of convenience foods, home baking skills are flourishing, though the preference has shifted from large cakes to tray bakes. Here is an unsurpassed favourite, especially when made with a delicate flaky pastry.

Flaky Pastry:
140g/5oz firm butter or margarine, grated
175g/6oz flour
pinch salt
iced water

Filling:
110g/4oz butter
80g/3oz sugar
225g/8oz currants
pinch spice
1 lemon, rind and juice
1 large apple, grated
1 slice bread, crumbled

Makes 20

Freeze butter or margarine for half an hour before grating. Sift flour and salt, then add butter or margarine and, using a palette knife, mix into flour. Add iced water until a dough is formed. Wrap and chill in fridge. Put all filling ingredients in a saucepan and bring to boiling point. Set aside to cool.

Preheat oven to gas mark 6, 200°C, 400°F. Roll out half the pastry very thinly and line a swiss roll tin. Pour on currant filling, spreading evenly, then cover with the rest of the pastry. Glaze with egg or milk. Bake for 30 minutes or until light gold in colour. Dust with caster sugar and cut into squares when cool.

DESSERTS

Apple Tart

The fat in the pastry for this pie should be half butter and half lard as this gives a good flavour; however, all butter may be used if wished. A light touch when rubbing in is essential and everything should be kept cool. The pastry should be allowed to 'rest' for half an hour in a cool place before rolling out.

Pastry:
250g/8oz plain flour
125g/4oz fat
pinch salt
iced water

Filling:
4 or 5 medium cooking apples
2 tbsp brown sugar
3 or 4 cloves (optional)

Rub the cold fat into the sieved flour in a large bowl. When it looks like fine breadcrumbs add two or three tablespoonfuls of iced water to bind, mixing with a round-bladed knife. Knead lightly and allow to rest before rolling out.

Line a 9 inch/ 25 cm metal pie dish with half the pastry. Peel and thinly slice the apples and put on the pastry base. Sprinkle the sugar over. Roll out the rest of the pastry as a lid, dampening the base around the edge to help it stick. Cut a vent in the top and bake near the top of the oven for 30 minutes at gas mark 7, 425°F, 220°C.

Serve cold with cream or hot with Custard Sauce.

Custard Sauce

A basic Custard Sauce is simple to make and a lovely accompaniment to any fruit tart or crumble.

2 tsps cornflour
575ml/1 pint milk
1-2 egg yolks
a few drops of vanilla essence
25g/1oz caster sugar

Blend the cornflour with a little of the milk. Put the remainder of the milk to heat in a saucepan. Cream the yolks, blended cornflour mix, vanilla essence and sugar together in a bowl.

Pour the heated milk into the bowl, stirring continuously. Rinse the saucepan in cold water then pour the custard mixture back into it.

Cook gently for three to four minutes stirring continuously until it has reached the required thickness but do not boil.

Blackberry Sorbet

A fresh fruit sorbet is a delightfully refreshing culmination to any meal. As a method of preserving the taste of a warm autumn into the depths of winter this simply-made sorbet is second to none. From late August to mid October wild blackberries can be picked from bushes by the side of country roads throughout Ireland. A wet summer followed by a warm, dry autumn will ensure a bumper crop.

500g/1lb fresh blackberries
125g/4oz sugar
125ml/¼ pint water
2 egg whites

Clean the blackberries thoroughly and remove stalks. Liquidise the fruit in a blender and strain through a sieve. Dissolve the sugar in the water and boil for about 5 minutes to make a syrup. Add the blackberries and boil for a further minute.

When the liquid has cooled, fold it into stiffly beaten egg whites. Freeze in an ice-cream machine or in ice cube trays in the freezer compartment of a fridge. If the latter is used, the mixture should be stirred about once an hour to prevent large ice crystals developing.

Gooseberry Crumble

This dish is an easily prepared and economical dessert, especially at the time of year when gooseberries are plentiful. The basic method can be used for other fillings, such as rhubarb, apple or apple and blackberry.

250g/8oz self-raising flour
125g/4oz soft brown sugar
125g/4oz butter
1kg/2lb gooseberries
200g/6oz caster sugar

Using your fingertips, rub in the butter lightly into the flour in a large bowl. When it is like fine breadcrumbs mix in the brown sugar.

Top and tail the berries and cover with the crumble mixture in an oven-proof dish, pressing the surface down lightly.

Bake for 45 minutes in the centre of a pre-heated oven at gas mark 4, 350°F, 180°C. Serve hot with cream or Custard Sauce (*see page 79*).

Apple Pie

This is how the best baker in my neighbourhood makes this universal family favourite. It combines the tartness of Bramleys, a couple of Cox's Pippins and, following the old books, a quince for superb flavour.

Shortcrust Pastry:
225g/8oz self raising flour
pinch salt
50g/2oz white pastry fat
50g/2oz good quality margarine
1 egg, beaten

Filling:
450g/1lb Bramley apples, peeled, cored and thinly sliced
225g/8oz Cox's Pippins, peeled, cored and thinly sliced
1 quince, grated (optional)
3 tbsp (heaped) sugar
nutmeg or cloves, grated
caster sugar to dust

Sift the flour and salt into a large mixing bowl. Cut the fat and margarine into small cubes and rub into the flour until the mixture resembles breadcrumbs. Mix the egg with a little water, reserve some to use as a glaze, and use the rest to bind the flour into a dough. Then wrap and chill in the fridge for 30 minutes.

Preheat oven to gas mark 6, 200°C, 400°F, warm a baking sheet, and grease and line a 24cm/9inch pie dish.

Roll out a little more than half the pastry on a floured surface and line the pie dish. Place apples and quince (if using) into the dish and add sugar and a little freshly grated nutmeg or cloves. Roll out the rest of the pastry to form a lid.

Brush the rim of the pastry base with water and place the lid on top. Seal and flute edges and make a few slits in the lid to allow steam to escape. Glaze with reserved egg and sprinkle with caster sugar.

Place pie dish on the warmed baking sheet and bake for 30 minutes. Serve with cream.

Rhubarb Fool

A fruit fool is a simple and delicious dessert, rich and creamy – but not overly so.

6-8 plump sticks of rhubarb
125g/4oz sugar
small knob of butter
250ml/½ pint whipping cream

Cut the rhubarb into chunks and sweat with the sugar and butter over a low heat until cooked but not mushy. Liquidise or pass through a food mill.

When cold, fold into stiffly-whipped cream. Allow to set in the fridge and serve with Lady finger or Boudoir biscuits.

Apple or **Gooseberry Fool** is made in exactly the same way, except that in the case of gooseberries the purée should be sieved to remove pips. It may be necessary to adjust sugar to taste.

Kerry Apple Cake

This cake does not keep very well, but that is not usually a problem, as you can be sure it will disappear very quickly! It is best eaten warm with cream or Greek-style yoghurt, and it is also perfect with cheese.

175g/6oz butter
175g/6oz caster sugar
2 eggs, beaten
225g/8oz self-raising flour
2 medium cooking apples, peeled, cored and chopped
1 tsp lemon rind
2 tbsp demerara sugar
pinch cinnamon
pinch nutmeg

Preheat oven to gas mark 4, 180°C, 350°F, and grease and line a 900g/2lb loaf tin.

Cream butter and sugar. Gradually add eggs and flour. Stir in apples and lemon rind.

Pour into the tin and sprinkle with sugar and spices. Bake for 1-1½ hours.

Country Rhubarb Cake

Both my parents ate this as children, dished straight out of the pot oven. The fruit and sugar would boil out around the sides, resulting in the gooey, syrupy cake they remember as a heavenly treat. The scone dough is quicker to make than pastry and absorbs the lovely juices better.

Scone Dough:
340g/12oz plain flour
½ tsp baking soda
pinch salt
50g/2oz caster sugar
80g/3oz butter
1 egg
175ml/6fl oz buttermilk

Filling:
700g/1½lb rhubarb, roughly chopped
200-250g/7-9oz sugar
white of 1 egg, whisked
caster sugar to dust

Preheat oven to gas mark 4, 180°C, 350°F, and grease a 25cm/10inch deep pie dish.

Sieve flour, baking soda and salt into a mixing bowl. Add caster sugar and rub in butter. In a separate bowl, beat the egg together with the buttermilk and gradually add this to the flour until a dough is formed.

Knead lightly on a floured surface and divide dough into two. Roll out one half and use it to line the pie dish. Fill the dish with the rhubarb and sprinkle with the sugar. Roll out the remaining dough to form a pastry lid. Brush the rim of the pastry base with water and put on the lid. Glaze with the whisked egg white and sprinkle with caster sugar.

Make steam slits in the lid and bake for 50-60 minutes or until the crust is lightly browned and the fruit is soft. This pie is also delicious if made with apples.

DRINKS AND CONFECTIONERY

Irish Coffee

¼ cup hot, strong, black coffee
½ tsp sugar
1 large measure Irish whiskey
1-2 tbsp double cream

Fill a stemmed whiskey glass with hot water then throw out, refilling it with boiling water. Throw this out, fill the glass somewhat more than half full with coffee and add sugar to taste. Stir to dissolve, then add the whiskey. Pour the cream over the back of a spoon to float on top.

Drink the hot liquid through the cool cream. If double cream is not available use lightly-whipped single (whipping) cream.

Hot Whiskey

A 'Hot Whiskey', also known as 'hot Irish' or just 'punch', is a favourite winter drink in Irish pubs.

boiling water
1-2 tsp sugar
1 large measure Irish whiskey
slice of lemon
2 or 3 whole cloves

Heat a stemmed whiskey glass as for Irish Coffee. Pour in fresh boiling water to more than half full, dissolve sugar to taste, add the whiskey, a slice of lemon and the cloves. Serve at once.

Yellowman

Did you treat your Mary Ann
to some dulse and yellowman,
At the Auld Lammas Fair in Ballycastle-O?

Dulse is a purple edible seaweed. I remember buying it at a penny a bag as a child when sweets were hard to get at. It can also be stewed for a couple of hours and eaten as a vegetable or with oatcakes. Dulse is something of an acquired taste but Yellowman is a different matter all together. This toothsome, honeycombed, sticky toffee is traditionally sold at the Auld Lammas Fair at the end of August.

500g/1lb golden or corn syrup
250g/8oz brown sugar
1 tbsp butter (heaped)
2 tbsp vinegar
1 tbsp baking soda

In a large saucepan slowly melt together all the ingredients except the baking soda. Do not stir. Boil until a drop hardens in cold water (240°F, 190°C on a sugar thermometer).

Stir in the baking soda. The toffee will immediately foam up as the vinegar releases the gas from the baking soda. Pour out onto a greased slab and while just cool enough to handle fold the edges towards the centre and pull repeatedly until the whole is a pale yellow colour. Allow to cool and harden in a greased tin and break into chunks with a toffee hammer – or anything else that comes to hand.

Acknowledgements

The publisher would like to thank the following for permission to reproduce work in copyright:

Page   6   © istockphoto.com / Floor S

Page 16   © istockphoto.com / Curt Pickens

Page 22   © istockphoto.com / Kelly Cline

Page 28   © istockphoto.com / Kelly Cline

Page 38   © istockphoto.com / Jack Puccio

Page 56   © istockphoto.com / bluestocking

Page 72   © istockphoto.com / Cheryl Casey

Page 76   © istockphoto.com / Alain Couillaud

Page 88   © Appletree Press

Index

Index